for the ones that wake me up at night
for those that sit in my father's chair
for the ancestors
for the gone too soon
Sandra Bland, Aiyanna Jones, Renisha McBride,
Rekia Boyd, Eric Garner, Mike Brown,
Eric Harris, Trayvon Martin, Oscar Grant,
the countless and oft nameless others
for their blood in my pen, for their mothers,
for their tears in my throat
and their rage in my heart,
the fire they put under my ass,
and the engine they made of my feet.
for all that made me rise from slumber...

and fight

Jasmine,

Thanks for the support and all your organizing!

Cheers?

SLEEPER CELL

BY

Michael "Quess?" Moore

NEXT LEFT PRESS
ASCENSION, LA

Sleeper Cell
published in the United States of America by
Next Left Press
Ascension, LA 70734
Copyright © 2016 Michael "Quess?" Moore

ISBN-13: 978-0996237499
ISBN-10: 0996237496

cover & interior art by Rontherin Ratliff
www.rontherin.com

author photo by New Orleans People Project

layout & book design by Geoff Munsterman
www.nextleftpress.com

SECOND PRINTING

the watch list

sleeper cell

upon the horizon
the rising of slain tribes
an army of apparitions
vaporous wisps of flame
at their fringe
are but smoke
plumes from the fire

at their core
indigo hearts beat
bleeding into the dreams of the living
for ether is the blood of ghosts
galvanized into electro
magnetic waves of consciousness

that draw a rising tide
of risen sleepers
imprisoned keepers
of long quelled flames

rekindled in kind
in kinsmen through thyme
and this is our season
to unearth truth like treason
from each root to each region
of a family tree ablaze

we are branches of cinder
and leaves of small embers
that yet still re:member
our indigo centers

to touch us with tender
awareness will render
recipient senses defenseless
and splintered

with change that remains
like a pain that sustains
but births a new form
like the Earth after rains

what blossoms from chains
are vines old as thyme
as aged as old sages
with wisdom their wine

O ye altered beasts of burden
rise from your graves
now dawns a new genesis
you are no longer slaves

once upon a distant sun

these words
are the broken ceramics
unearthed from long lost
trade routes of Kemetic sands
reminders of a buried truth
3rd eye be using the shards
of my shattered past to carve
out peepholes into my future

once upon a distant sun
eye crafted golden chariots of war
engraved with blueprints
of their construction
as instructions for my unborn

knowing when the gold
rusted into the muddled brown
of our future decay
when our one day children
were mastered by those
they once mastered

the curving lines of ancient
glyphs would arch angles
of memory into the divine
light of the world
from whence they came

Afrimerican manboy

see me
i'm an archaeologist
with fumbly fingers
i often go forging
for the fossils of my forefathers
only to find the path
blocked by my own trembling bones
too shaky to hold the weight
of my own ancestry
shoulders still trying to muster
strength to bear/bare
the burden of my own inheritance
i'm an American boy of an African man
somewhere between modern neuroses
& age old gris gris
be trynna pull the kente cloth
out of my tapestry
but it always comes out stained
red, white & blue
but i suppose
anything less wouldn't be true

Yakub's Children

they came back to us
a different color
strangely shaped
hair where there was none
growing limply, falling downward

over pallid flesh
eyes cold & blue
as the sea they sailed in on
or pale green as chameleon skin

noses pointed as their gaze
sharp as spears
narrow as their lips
disappearing into their faces

all white
the color of death
their teeth brown with decay
danger & ocean under their fingers

these lost men
with such fierce intention
their eyes glazed over with mischief
desperation beneath their tongues

they came to us
we knew not of their origin
or their departure
or that this was indeed their return

these lost men
broken in their bravado
cocksure in their waywardness
our long ago children

we embraced them
with harms half closed

5

when teaching the children
of the enslaved...

proceed with caution
know that they know
not what they do
they have never woken from the centuries

> long slumber their ancestors
> were forced into
> the rusted shackles round their brains
> will resist yore tongue's tutelage
> no matter how razor sharp

trying to free a slave
that does not know he is one
is like trying to unleash a rabid dog
that has only known the hands of an abusive master

> do not be alarmed by the growls
> nor the bites
> they're just doing what scared animals do

the 7 years
I spent as an educator
flood my mind's rearview mirror
with a packed hallway
of young brown bodies

their wanting faces & hungry eyes
their arms outstretched in yearning
until they age

> & something seals their mouths
> the light in their eyes runs for cover
> their palms clasp close to their sides
> shrivel into fists tight as paws

the laughter mutates from cotton soft hum
to thorny toothed cackle
as they sharpen their edges to claw
the blunt realities that await them

the children of the enslaved know
a bit more than we give them credit for
more than they give themselves credit for
know the vice grip of adulthood
will noose their adolescent thoughts

before they ever know free range

know their lives will know the limits
of their parent's lives
& their parent's parent's lives
if they don't fight for free reign

yet too bound by fear
of the same pallid hands
that sent they granddaddy's
& they granddaddy's granddaddy's

to the cotton fields at 12
up the river at 13
to the bottom of it by 14

to try to buoy their way up
from where their ancestors started

cause they're still here
still huddling under back doorways

no one has to carve for them
anymore

Education

Education... root word... educe
interchangeable with ... elicit ... evoke ... draw out...

like water from a well... sap from a tree...
                                    or that masterpiece hidden
                                    in marble brought to life
                          by the hands of the master sculptor

these children   are clay
in our hands   we be the masters
                                        of this ceremony...
                                        both crafters & creators

                    so you best believe every time
                    we step into that classroom
                    'Their Eyes are Watching God'

so pardon me if you will
but I take issue with a God
                        that don't look like me
                        dictating the discourse

in an age of virtual reality
globalization corporate
commodification genetic
engineering stem-cell
cloned sheep—it seems

                    a bit of that weird science
                    has leaked into the classroom...

                    I mean... what's with all the cross-pollination?

in October of 2009, a group of teachers imported
from the Philippines pressed charges for
being treated like & paid no better than
indentured servants

my only question...
what the hell were they doing here in the first place?

I'm here

apt & completely capable
of teaching children that look
just like I did 20 years ago

& now walk a similar path

But in the political ponzi game
that is Post-Katrina New Orleans
it's bigger than books & study baby
EDUCATION IS BIG BUSINESS

Unions shut down wholesale
veteran teachers fired
before they can cash in
pensions—God forbid healthcare
Prison beds
forecast by the amount of children
at grade level

does it get more insidious than that...?

whatever best supports the bottom line
like the Board of Ed's keeping strange
bedfellows with big companies
taking tips from Walmart
on how to run a school

& with all the corporate sponsors
feeding the average charter school
& the high-end-usually-right-wing-think tanks
designing their agendas... it's no surprise
when Sam Walton himself is on the board

in some of his final words
infamous economist Milton Friedman
said "Katrina...was a tragedy"
but at the same time...

9

"an opportunity to radically reform the educational system"

that's bullshit old white man-ese
for wipe out the New Orleans Public School System
& replace it with independent charter schools

wanna know who the charters answer to...

just follow the money...
probably the same
right wing think tanks
who conjured a test to LEAP
over our kids' heads while steadily
claiming they won't leave 'em behind
same old moneyed banks and good ole boy
companies who held our great- great-
great-great grandmothers
in chains
...
so what's to be made of all this 'good-hearted' altruism, huh?

penance for ancestral pains?

like giving a Band-Aid to an AIDS patient
good luck covering the wounds
hope this cheap amalgamation of
gauze & adhesive tape don't slip
like sloppy seconds over
the festering sores
good luck with the facts...
hope the textbook prognosis
works out for ya li'l buddy...

perhaps it'll plaster perfectly
over the pathos we
supplied in surplus

these wounds, my child
...are age old
even older than the wilted
buildings we house them in
but sometimes...

10

as though the buildings were
symptoms themselves
the chipping of lead based painting
on 80 year old walls sounds like
looks like broken English

a barb wired vice grip on a muzzled mouth
a poisonous laminate atop petrified wood

our indigenous breath once blew
linguistic form from a shapeless void
now we're painted a plethora of platitudes
minstreled in misnomers
Gifted & Nigger...
Special Needs ... Trouble Child
our children...

our children are a poisoned harvest
ripened out of season...
who will tend this garden better...
than those who sprouted from it themselves...?

Before the Cement Settles

Once upon a world in a time called Brooklyn
I grew up amongst a beautiful breed
of blessed brown boys & girls
cradled in the brick & mortar safety
of a red school house set atop impenetrable gravel
we grew up on & out of the concrete
then adopted it as our namesake

I'm a man now

yet still a card carrying member
of that Concrete Generation
who never cared much for sentiment that danced
outside the chalk lines of what we crafted as cool
& if you didn't know what that was
you were just another fool never to be pitied
within the heartlessness of a city that pollinated
the same grounds that its children sprouted from
with the very vials of crack that pawned so many
of our parents to the reaper

no wonder the grimness of our grimaces
labeled as society's menaces
with shadows cast cross our existences
leaving our inner light diminishing
no wonder the rusted silver lining
on clouds already grey

the cynical grins
a token of how truths & lies contend
& in the balance blend
on the beleaguered brown
faces of America's bastard breed

no wonder callous hearts grew
hard as the concrete we walked on
but before we ever learned
to pave bitterness into bitumen

before we cemented childhood pains
into gargoyle faced adolescence
& learned to concretize tears into brittle
shards of rock that barely ever
stumbled from their ducts
...we were children
dressed in little white gowns & white caps
with red tassels to celebrate entry into a world
of false hope & falser doctrine
at our kindergarten graduation
blessed brown boys & girls
red brick schoolhouse
& the voice... of a goddess
...
she told us that we were the future
that we would one day lead
but should first be taught well
& shown the beauty we possessed inside
gave us a sense of pride
pretty mocha brown angel lady
strangers said my mother looked like her
walking me thru Brooklyn streets
in skin New Orleanian caramel
grippin' my hands tight amongst jackals that lurked parallel
kinda like the mocha brown angel lady
who cradled my youth with her voice
despite the demons that lurked parallel

who knew what hell tarried
well beneath the surface
that microphones never heard
that cameras never captured
all we saw... was the face of an angel
all we heard... the voice of a goddess
who told us that the greatest love of all
was learning to love our selves
we sang her words... recited them like scripture
she's gone now
back to the heavenly graces from whence she came
& I only pray that she learned
to practice what she preached

13

Dear Whitney,

you faded away before our eyes far too soon
left us long before your time. not February 11, 2012,
but the day your body ceased to be temple to guard
& turned cage to crack out of. the last time I saw you
on television, you were a frazzled manic wreck
your motions as scattered as your speech
your time melting away like a Dali-esque clock
into a Pollock splattered mess of a life...

a work of sabotaged art

mocha goddess of our youth
shattering before our eyes
like crackling porcelain
"drifting away in your skin..."
perhaps missing the love of distant kin

we loved you Whitney
but like your mother's cringing
face shadowed in shame
at too many an award show
we could hardly bear to watch
the circus freak you had become

love and shame
rarely occupy the same space
they wax atomic when they meet
the explosive outcome renders us numb
left to gloss over our apathy ever after
with snide jokes and clever laughter
cut from the bowels of our bitterness

so we clowned your drug addiction
in the same vein as our inoculated innocence
our cynicism a vaccine
against the sickness of soured sentiments

cause we'd been had one too many times
been the brunt of this bad joke once too often
all our heroes and she-roes quarantined to coffins
our patriarchs & matriarchs minstreled as buffoons
left dead on hotel balconies
or caught smoking crack in the rooms
for every cookie cutter Kodak moment
there's a clandestine conspiracy that looms...adjacent

...slave children in the attic
dead bodies in the basement
Hollywood starlet
but on the low be free basin'
The Land of the Free
a Dictatorship of Free Masons
government granting the crack
that lead to your fall from grace and
it was all too sick a reality show
to watch without a wince
so when it came to your illness
no words could we mince

reminded us too much of our father's cold corpses
old uncles leanin' against corner stores for support
my cousin's red eyes thru the peephole at 4 in the morning
asking for gas money & he don't even own no car...

funny
not funny
as your existence became
before our chuckling mouths
laughing over the pain
tap dancing over the shame

the past now crystallized
thru our blurry eyes
& as the smoke clears
along with our tears
we can but glance at the surface
glimpse of goddess that you gave us
& bid your great spirit adieu

as we find remorse

not so much for the jokes we cracked to cope
but for the coke we cooked to crack
the joke it made of your life
& so many of ours...

& how easily we fell for that punch line

Dear Whitney,

your song remains, evergreen
will sing us through seasons to come
we don't know what torturous angles
broke your heavenly wings angel
turned your temple to cage
you felt you had to flee, but your spirit
has finally escaped its vessel
and is from now... to life everlasting
                                        free

smoke signals
(for the Scott brothers... and all the brothas)

*On January 21, 2013, as per usual, MLK Day in New Orleans concluded
in a violent shooting. This was my attempt to speak to the shooter.*

I.

once upon a time. blunts upon they mind. youngins on the line
'tween they life & death. that's when I was a young Brooklyn boy that
came down to NOLA where the teens would fight to death. Katrina
swiped a rest in peace sign all across the street signs. only memories
ignite what's left. but even everything in my rear view from 9th ward to
Clearview lookin' like a scene of trifling mess. heartbeats stop due
to stifling stress or on a dark street shot or from knife to chest.
youngin's with no options pitchin from they spot on the block with they
glock livin life or death...

II.

last night on the 6 o' clock evening news,
a map of my city stretched across the TV
screen like the body of a diseased patient
pockmarked in dots
like an AIDS victim in the 80's
a sickness had torn loose in the metropolis
leaving only red spots on a digital map
to symbolize the slain

sterile as neuroscientists
                    newscasters delivered the diagnosis:

"There were 17 shootings over the MLK Birthday weekend
bringing the total to 33 in the last 5 days.
Most of the perpetrators ranging from ages 15-21."

the words echoed through my mind
like clicking heels down
the halls of an insane asylum
took me back to a small room
9x5x9, age 14, caged like an animal
stab wound carved in my left arm

the shape of an eye:
center of my storm
pink pulp staring up at me
reminding me how ugly I was
dormant fury stirring like cloud formations
on the distant shores of my chest
echoing how I'd gotten there
time immeasurable in front of me
whispering of things to come
& from whence I'd come...

III.

dear brother,

there was a time before western shores when we walked/ side by side through life... before we learned to sprint to death/ when the endless list of victims was bereft of our names/ when our heads were left clear of each other's aim/ when we didn't claim manhood based on how much we maimed/ when we chose love over hate, trust over trickery/ embracing bloodlines over running from our history/ but that time is gone now/ we live here... in these divided states... with hearts & minds that reflect it/ I once saw myself in you but now we're just broken mirrors trying to figure out each other's missing parts/ without enough knowledge of our own/ in a land we've never quite been able to call home/ so we be lost on misplaced missions fueled by angst-ridden ambition in search of our long lost thrones/ some found in suburban homes, others in Big Bodies on spinning chrome/ but a man can only run from his past so long until it cycles back to him/ can only hate for so long until it withers him hollow/ halts the beat of the heart—stopped—replaces it with machine parts/ no wonder you gravitate to metal... regurgitating bullets like shrapnel of an inner explosion/ as dazzled denizens belch out gun smoke questions from slack jawed mouths...

IV.

how did it feel when the bullet left the chamber?
when the rocket exploded thunderbolts from your palms...

18

as you set worlds bewildered ablaze, were you Zeus almighty
casting lightning into the terrified village?
did you possess the power of 10 men?
mincing mortals into scattering ants
at the elephant hooved thump of death
charging through the urban jungle...

how did the gun sit in your hands?
was the cold callous steel a coffin for fear?
did you hear your Grandmothers whispers in your ear?
were you her Moses of the Bible parting Red Seas
of enemies' arteries beneath the war-torn terrain of flesh?

...paving pathways... to a promise land of...

where does your road lead?
who promised you no tomorrow? why did you believe them?
is this your righteous indignation, your holy vengeance?
are you God himself in flesh spewing venom?
belligerent bastion of youthful rage born of the mouth of babes
demon in basket spawned at river's mouth
prodigal pathos come home to haunt slums of New Egypt

a raucous remix on a redemption song maybe
a once righteous revolution gone awry
feasting on its own fingers before it can form a fist
or hold it up...
chewing its poisoned tongue into bloody
oblivion before it finds the words to speak...
are you my child... an antiquated anguish
spilling like spoiled milk into the lap of modernity?

do we detest the stench of reminiscence inborn in your scowl?
your brazen eyes screaming
louder than the pack of wolves you run lonely in...
are you aware?
of the storms that gather round you... within you...
do you know how powerful you are?
how great the monsoon in your chest
to the small fire in your palms
attracting heat to match your misplaced passion
in the form of glock 9's, cops, crime
and poor rehashing of gangster movie plotlines

V.

so they have regarded you as suspect
looked at you like bomb threat
as perhaps they should
you are highly flammable walking cinder
ancestral ember born of the fire
of your fore bearer's dreams
oppressors speak kerosene in your presence
& wonder why situations wax explosive
don't let them throw water on you
it would only prove corrosive to your development

tho the creasing of flames
beneath your eyelids
may prove necessary for survival
your power is sun flare
you won't be welcome at every table
it'll be there loss when you depart
walk...
well & remain true   to only your heart
your ancestors live there

they told me never to take no wooden nickels
so I've invested my life in restoring you, us, we
to the golden standard we fell from
don't make the mistakes I did
ambivalence will get you nowhere
but trapped between your own
heartbeats like gunshots
triggered by your instincts—
trust them!

they craft your truth in the shape of your spirit's shadow
& in that dark place, you'll find more direction
than any man-made compass could ever provide
inside, cradled in a nest of your grandmother's wisdom
guarded by the shards of your father's shattered pride
there's a reflection of all that glowed
from the wells in your mother's eyes
do you remember...
who you were... before your fire
... consumed you?

fratricide

when your younger brother's smirking eyes
find humor in the latest black body snuff film

when he looks at you
as though he's found a new toy
& asks if you've seen the latest one
where the 16 year old boy from Chicago
gets a bullet for each year
running away knife in hand
from an army of cops

               PCP flowing through the boy's body
like a river to an ocean falsely named freedom
through a battle torn wasteland of a teenaged body
when your brother sees the river in the wasteland
blames the boy for running towards it

the small black boy's retreat
    a scared squirrel's scurry
        from a pack of rabid jackals
           when he blames the squirrel for its sudden
               movements & not the dogs for their drooling
             fangs their ravenous mouths
                   in front of unworthy prey

               when he writes the boy
             a second death sentence
           deems him undeserving of protest
    says we black folks waste too much time
        running behind the unworthy

the too much slouching pants
    cornbread in hand in hot pursuit of escape from
        the too much running river of narcotic
           flooding the senses for us to be trying
             to make sense of their senseless black lives
                 it will not matter

that you & he were born of the same womb
were once seeds from the same inconstant gardener of a father
that you bloomed through the same Brooklyn brick & mortar
at the hands of a woman who tilled your character
like precious soil in the middle of a war zone

        when your brother says Laquan is not worthy
          you will ask him if he was worthy

                  if you were worthy

           when one night on Canal Street
     unmarked cars surrounded your mother's van
          told you & him to get the fuck out
     before they Russian Rouletted your future
          into the typical black oblivion
         & when the undercover cops left
     after releasing the binds from your wrist
       & your bodies from the concrete
     told you *You're lucky it wasn't worse*

were you worthy

the night he was too high
& you too drunk to give a damn
bout some invisible police line
cause Jada Kiss was in the building behind it
& you'd be damned if some asshole cop
was gonna stand between you
& your college boy frolic of a night
even if it meant spending
the night behind bars

                  was he worthy

         when you both skipped the invisible
     line trying to hop the Marta in Atlanta
      he escaped narrowly, you got caught
       & took the charge for both of you

was his brother worthy

when a year after their father's death
older brother turned

Molotov cocktail in warzone
city streets exploded into
attempted murderer at age 14

when your brother
finds humor in the snuffing
out of a body that could have been his
or yours

your heart will clench like a fist
will lay siege to all the blood in your body
will make you hungry for the blood of another
even if it resembles your own

you will remember that annoying little kid
that laughed too soon at all the wrong jokes
before he learned to seal his soft
in the concretized mores of the street
guild them in the cast iron conformity
of what it meant to be young, black & boy

you will remember how your hands became
welding hammers trying to beat the soft out of him
to pound his frame into
a more acceptable version of black & boy
you will look into his now crooked smirk
his jaded eyes bruised in jaundice & see
you have succeeded

When They Came for Me

i was all flailing limbs

bulging eyes

staring thru midnight black

was still frame
captured in lantern's light
my silhouette cast
on southern tree canvas

foreshadowing my death
was fleeing phantom
of the antebellum opera
shaky fingers   moistened
palms

trembling teeth
mumbling 23rd psalms

yay, tho i spoke my mother's mantras
i found no peace in the valley
my hunters crafted for me

my sweaty brow
a furrowed forest
above awe struck eyes
white as moonlight

i ran
...
i ran scared

squirrelly tremors in darkness
born of king's blood and
lion's heart
reduced to
conniving rat scurrying
through throes of survival

                              stripped of claws and fangs
                stripped of mane and pride

          my cubs   sold at master's whim
        my growth   at the limits of master's whip
      my humanity   blocked on stages of
human auction

                    when they came for me
                    i was not surprised
            i have known nothing other than

quick footfalls at bang of firing metal
shriek shrill at crack of leather lash
swift silence at snap of dangling rope
                              i have never known still

i have only known...
            RUUUUUUUUNNN!!!

Post Racial America:
A Children's Story

We need to have a conversation about race...
silence *turns page*

We need to have a conversation about race.
silence *turns page*

We need to have a conversation about race!
silence *turns page*

We need to have a conversation about—BANG!
Gunsmoke *silence* *turns page*

We need to have a conversation about—BANG! BANG!
Gunsmoke *blood* *silence* *turns page*

We need to have a conversation—BANG! BANG! BANG!
Gunsmoke *blood* blood* *screams* *silence* *turns page*

We need to have a—BANG! BANG! BANG! BANG!
Gunsmoke * blood* * blood* * blood* *screams* *silence* *turns page*

We need to have—BANG! BANG! BANG! BANG! BANG!
Gunsmoke * blood* * blood* * blood* * screams* *screams* *silence*
turns page

We need to—BANG! BANG! BANG! BANG! BANG! BANG!
Gunsmoke * blood* * blood* * blood* * blood* * screams* *screams*
silence *turns page*

We need—BANG! BANG! BANG! BANG! BANG! BANG! BANG!
Gunsmoke * blood* * blood* * screams* * blood* * screams* *blood*
silence *turns page*

We—BANG! BANG! BANG! BANG! BANG! BANG! BANG! BANG!
Gunsmoke *silence* *turns page*

America, what's in your name?

America,

If my name is part your name
so much so in fact that you could fit me inside you...

If I am Eric a
6 foot tall 300 pound brown man
skin Mississippi mud
voice Italian accented
as any New York native
does my perfect blend of melting pot
miscegenation not Garner enough respect
for you to not choke me to death in broad daylight?
to not matador your manic
nightmares of me out of plain view

if I am Sean
wedding bells ringing in my near future
will it buy me enough time for you to not permanently
alter my chances at a happily ever after?

If I am Michael
meaning messenger of God
and am born Brown, but my message is muted
by the bullets of a white cop
before it ever gets to mature
does anyone hear the body drop?
or does it just rot
like a post-modern dream
deferred into a blur
of concrete & what else is new?

If I am Oscar
worthy of a glimpse
at the main stage of life
will it Grant me a nomination

of human
of son
of father
of worthy
of next breath
& second chance
to kiss my wife
& lay my daughter down to bed at night
without you puppeteering her nightmares
for years to come?

do you sleep well at night
knowing that my mother never will?

do you rest peacefully
knowing you have denied me
the chance to do anything but?

America,

what dark phantoms creep in the underbelly of your dream?
what ocean of skeletons tap-dance round your bed at night?
what terror do you dress black bodies in
that we all turn to bullseyes under your scope?

how rigid must be my walk
how docile the smile & timid the eyes
to not boil your bloodlust?
& jostle your murderous knee jerk?

how articulate must be my speech
to match the diction of a genocidal derelict?

what you gon teach my kids America?
bout grit... bout pull yourself up by ya bootstraps?
when you pulled your empire
out of the ashes & dust
of bloodied black bodies for centuries?

what you gon teach me
bout non-violence—bout turn the other cheek?
well with all that blood plastered to your hands & teeth

you owed yourself a National State of Emergency a long time ago

but who is to save you?
when it is the long arms of your own law
that strangle your lifespan shorter everyday
that make ritual sacrifice of your own
citizens everyday

where go these black bodies
that your law leaves lifeless
to what God of fear?
to what angry gnashing teeth mouth
of hell born fury?

America

if my name is part your name
you are a murderer of your own tongue
your teeth, the jagged edged knife devouring your speech
your truth, a blood soaked venom your children choke on

you are a sadomasochistic suicide letter
a death wish feeding on itself

you can not cut off your round nose
to spite your pale face
cannot amputate the Africa from your American body
we will haunt you
like phantom limb

will be the missing blues in a rock you can no longer cull blood from

we
who are born to bronze
under the warm eye of sun
deemed obscene if we don't
bleach our black to oblivion

we
of rhythmic tongue
that dance circles
round yore dead end linear narrative
of murder death kill
of perpetual war and rumors thereof

we
who have always been there
to serve your whims America
to quench your blood thirst
& quell the hunger pangs in your beastly belly
while tap dancing across your fangs

only to find
lonely solace in your cavernous heart
an amphitheater of the depraved
waiting to feast on our brown skins

we will no longer dance for you
nor sing your song of death

what will become of you
when the minstrel leaves the theater?

when you are left
bereft of black
mammies and pickaninnies
to pluck the fear & boredom
from your cash cropped craniums

America,

if my name... is part your name
you are a continent of cacophonous consonants
that will collapse in my absence
once you vanquish the vowels

we will howl in the wind
reform our selves nebulous

rain our selves anew
to fertilize the tomorrows
our earth incubates for us

will wade in the waters of *her* womb
to be reborn in the wake of *your* absence
but we will no longer try to *fit*
inside of *you* America
you can spell out your death sentence

                                        alone

blood on the hands

i can mark my calendar
w/ the blood that stains your hands
can count the tics & tocs of my clock
in the cadavers you drop

what is time to you?

but a thing measured in black bodies
a dark abyss smothered in corpses
what is it that you seek when you run?
what is that you run from when you seek?

you who are born of frozen wombs
who know cold like second skin
& seek the warmth of other's sons
in the summer when their blood fills
the chalice of your unholy communion
your cup runneth over
with privilege & oblivion & blood
like wine spilled from strange fruit
rotted & twisted on the vine

the poisoned bloom of severed seeds
sown out of season
the seized suns & daughters
of dusted primordial orders
raised like cattle for slaughter

their hides singed
from regal bronze
to crimson bloodbath
till they turn up
yellow bellied in torpor
in this season of fall
into the coldest winter ever

your domain of ice & apathy
where your father's traditions
have forged your will iron
your eyes gilded & steadfast
in their narcissistic gaze

as the corpses pile
& the living spring
up in rebellion
for fear of another
blood hot summer

you remain steady
on your deadly course
chartered by the bloody
hands of father time...

each tic a collapsing corpse
a metronome marking your steps

as you run against the clock
like all them bloody footprints
won't catch up with you

Hands up

a sea of black hands go up
lifted to the sky in worship
in surrender
all the same
in ecstasy
or in drowning
all the same

what we know is
hands go up
to take away the pain
to lessen the weight
of the struggle called life
to clear the air of strife
& know the divinity of breath

"Hands up..."
"I can't breathe..."
the rallying cry of a godless generation
with no sweet chariot to call upon
Pizza Man don't even come to our block no mo'
for our faces are tarnished in tar
by the sins of another

our dreams feathered in false wings
reflecting the glow of Technicolor billboards
as we have repeatedly leapt
into short-lived flight
only to thump our clucking heads
on cinderblock glass ceilings
milky & opaque to our uplifted eyes
beholden before a false good...

...god...

was that God that we gazed upon?
in white robe & white skin perched
atop white cloud in endless white sky
was that heaven?

hovering above us from beyond
milky white cinder block glass
concealing all white board room
where the good clean alabaster man
delivered good clean alabaster speech
from behind unyielding podium
was that heaven?

that he went home to
with good clean alabaster wife
& family in good clean white house
with white picket fence
in good clean white suburb

were we black & dirty?

born into midnight sin
products of unholy environs
hell bound even when homebound
is that why Pizza Man don't come to our block no mo'?

but the cops do
like some manic band of guardian angels
in service of an eyeless god
come to repurpose our wrongness into whiteness
I mean our blackness into rightness
that we might be worthy
to worship at your temple
to sit at the pallid feet of your...

...godlessness...

your empire
has no god
all its standards are broken
its commandments crushed to dust
your temple is a marketplace
worthy of righteous ransack

but you have made yourself
deaf to reprimand

taken measures against your own redemption
preemptively struck down any black messiah
that might show you the mountaintop
beyond the valley of the shadow of death
that you have carved for yourself

& here we lie
in broken wing
trying to ferret our way out
the vice grip of have not
flutter plastered feathers
to a summit of false
light that yet burns still

the harvest

what a body be hands up back turned palms corner store candy sticky fingers round dime cigarettes legs in frazzled motion head ducking limbs in retreat neck noosed in arms or rope eyes a gap with fear cut narrow with suspicion eyes bloodshot rage eyes a window to nothing a no man's land behind the lens cause who knows who goes there in that sheet of midnight black in that veil of Mississippi mud earth say nothing good can come from all that dark say darkness be host of demons be devil's workshop no wonder they always idle, shiftless, drifting in and out of target's range fitting right in it like he do the description and ain't much to describe cause don't we already know what she look like? don't he always look the same? be she Mississippi mud or Georgia Red Clay a Tar Baby's black always blossoms into beast just more harvest for the feast...
     of souls

Obesity

usually when I eat bad I develop a knot
in my stomach that won't let me keep swelling
my belly without purging my insides. failure
to do so results in stomach pains in the short term
or a flabby gut in the long term. gluttony...

is the failure to check one's self in the pursuit of greed-fueled desires

the ravenous eye on defenseless prey
the salivating tongue
plunging fang into tender meat
tearing meat from limb to limb to shreds
the forgetful belch after the kill
the accrual of weight
repeat cycle. sometimes...

after enjoying a really good kill
i look at the scattered bones on my plate
& think Auschwitz. think Warsaw.
think Door of No Return & hungry ocean floor
think slaughtered buffalo & wonder...
how much meat does it take
to fill the belly of a beast
& will it even realize it's full before it bursts?

cause there had to be a time, some Trail of Tears time, some Midwest Bowl
full of Dust back in ya face time, some Amistad on your shores like so much
karmic regurgitation time, when the vomit in your mouth spoke to the knot in
your guts, when their conversation rippled beneath the folds in your beastly
belly & you questioned for at least a second how sustainable was this diet.
& how long could you last on it before the flesh & bones of rotting cadavers
started decaying your breath till you opened your mouth & everyone could
smell what was coming before you even spoke

So I'm touring the
Texas State Capitol...

...my small brown body cast against the canvas of tall white coliseums
reaching back centuries, I'm dwarfing in the bleached shadows of their history

where brown bodies like mine were but minor details in the portrait of American
destiny manifest only in the margins as footnotes on the pages of recorded history

but right now... right now my thoughts are of Brianna
Brianna, of light Latina hue & American college girl humor

she is a walking library of White Supremacist mythology
trapped in a mausoleum of Mestizo skin, Brianna

knowledgeable tour guide who just walked me & some 30
visitors through the pristine halls of the Capitol

the jokes glint off her tongue with irony
her commentary clashes with her culture

as she speaks of Texas history in the possessive, "We were defeated
by Mexico in the Battle of the Alamo in 1836," she says

"We rallied back 6 weeks later & won the Battle of San Jacinto
thereby founding the great state of Texas," she continues...

& I keep trying to figure out how she manages
to fit all her light brown *me*
inside of all that Western White *we*

how she minces memories of Moccasin shoe mamas
beneath the steel toes & steers of Lone Star boots
walking her across the marble floors of her oppressor's history

as she speaks, there's a festival going on in front of the capitol
her voice struggles to be heard above blaring sounds of Reggaeton

rhythms booming from the speakers outside
& I can't help but wonder if the cognitive dissonance inside
her head doesn't blare just as loudly

there are women, many of Brianna's hue, dancing to her people's music
I think they're doing Zuumba… or the Macarena… or some shit that English

words just fail to do justice & I'm wondering how she fails
to see the injustice in the story she's been paid to propagate

& can she hear her ancestors' rebuttal
thumping in the drums as they echo
through the halls of the Texas State Capitol—Brianna!

…can you hear your ancestors calling?

at the tour's end, an elderly white women asks Brianna
"What does the word Texas mean?"

She quickly replies, "It's a Cahto Indian word for friendship."
& I immediately want to look up the word friendship to see

if there's anything I missed, perhaps
there are etymological references to blood

splattered chieftains & Trails of Tears
maybe those are key ingredients
to lifelong bonds & i'm the oblivious one

or maybe

maybe Texas… like America… is just a really fucked up friend
the kind that vice grips your bones in its handshake until

your bones are ground to dust & your remains are left
to mix with the blood & sweat of capital gains to form

the watered down colors they use to paint
the monuments to *their* greatness
                              they'll etch your name in the edges
                    of their borders, shade you into their shadows

       as footnote   loser of the battle   vanquished foe turned mascot
              misguided tour guide through the halls of *their* history

never as foundation
as keeper of land before hostile takeover
as blood rites to this ground before oil rape

TEXAS!

if you are friendship

        ...then what do I call my enemies?

When the white Guy calls
your not quite girlfriend
a bitch and you remain silent...

It's not that you don't want to
- pulverize the blood from his skull
- gouge his eyes from their sockets
- pull the still beating heart from his pale chest
- & say *See! All Lives DO Matter, except yours fuckhead!*

It's not that you don't want to
- "beat that bitch with a bottle"
- plunge the remaining jagged edges into his throat
- & drag towards the bottom of his ears like he dragged for your
  not quite girlfriend

but see the way your social anxiety is set up
you were too deer in headlights of
smug white boy cynicism to see it coming
too caught in the crosshairs of his sarcasm to notice
the switchblade narcissism of the tongue wielding it

the darting blue snatch of his wife's eyes
chiming in with cheerleading smiles & featherweight banter
to charm you & your not quite girlfriend
the seemingly friendly volley of conversational cannon fodder
the back & forth of it all
while you watch words hop, skip & jump
over your head like a volleyball
game you're too short to play

you, all Brooklyn boy brick & mortar
all *I don't fuck with white folks like that anyway less they meet me*
  on my terms
all Macklemore gon need a dissertation
& a co-sign & a little bit of blood for the cause
fore I give him any street credit
all ½ Hotep, ⅖ Blipster, ⅗ analog boy in a Digital world
all perpetual manchild in the broken promise land
too socially awkward for most rooms you fit into
much less the ones you don't

& here you are
at a sports bar in New Orleans
you & your not quite girlfriend, one of a few tokens
in an otherwise good old white boy hipster affair
she trying to bridge the gap between her past & present
her former white roommate friend
& her down for the cause activist not quite boyfriend
& then this white man in the middle
hurling insults & jokes like they're the same thing
most of them leaping just above your head
you let them fly
even when your heart tells you
to make dead birds of them
to aim with precision & shoot his words lifeless
from the air he's contaminating them with

but then he says "bitch"
easy as asking for the check
& he's talking about your not quite girlfriend, who is black
& you know it's not the usual missile
didn't quite follow the trajectory of most projectiles you're used to
in Brooklyn, in Tallahassee, in New Orleans

what you're used to is "Beat that bitch with a bottle"
what you're used to is "Who you calling a Bitch!? U-N-I-T-Y..."
what you're used to is "I ain't Ice T & I ain't Ice Cube,
but I had to knock the brother out for being rude!"
what you're used to is call a black woman out her name
& in turn be named everything but a child of God
as you book tickets to the most remote island on the planet
OR prepare to write your own eulogy

what you've known
is 3½ decades on planet Earth
without that word ever
having grazed the ears of
a black woman in her presence
from the mouth of a man
much less a white one
& that man having lived to tell about it
with the same amount of blood in his body

43

so this white man's "bitch"
does not float past you like featherweight banter
it bursts like a nuclear bomb
like something small as pollen
just infiltrated the air in you
detonated & left everything hollow
you look into the face of your not quite girlfriend
a small wince & then she too
                                    hollow
the silence between you a mushroom cloud

you become the averted eye
contact between estranged lovers
the morning after massuh's hands
went places they ain't had no bidness
cept they did, cause both your bodies
have always been massuh's business

white man her friend's husband
at the other end of the table
carries on oblivious, business as usual
he all American ship at the Gulf of foreign territories
not expecting a rebuttal
you all Somalian pirate
sharpening the blade of your tongue
your anger rusting over beneath pursed lips

your anger the petrified wood of the oldest African tree
that has never known the blood of those Southern trees in America
that has never shouldered the weight of black corpses by white hands
but that longs desperately for this white man's weight
to be noosed to the ends of your limbs
vice gripped between your fingers
like your ancestors' necks to rope

want *him* to say "I can't breathe"
want to peer into the blue depths of his barren eyes
see if they ring as still water deep
as the sorrow presently consuming you

a sorrow deep as the Atlantic
& riddled with just as many bones

want to see if there's any soul
beneath all that empty in his eyes
think maybe you can choke it out of him

bring it to the surface

like a black body

resurrected

from the ocean floor

Wild Thing

Dear Max,

can you tell me "where the wild things go?"
after you put your fantasies to sleep
once you finish Joseph Conrading your way
through the heart of distant darkness

& return to comfortable sterility
in your suburban safe box home
what does your boyish imagination do
with all the yellow eyes
sharp teeth & menacing fangs
you subdued into submission
with the mere glare
of your brazen white boy stare?

where do the wild things go?

when unleashed from the bondage of your gaze...
no benevolent master left to sanction their laughter
to stamp their wiles with approval
chalk borders round their unkempt edges
& manicure their mania

when you are done with all the keeping Max
who keeps you?

Gentrification in 5 parts:
A play on the senses

what smells like lemon pledge
& bologna mixed with
a dash of gutter punk funk?

sounds like a churning coffee bean grinder
set to a backdrop of new construction
can't tell the difference between
the grind outside...
                     & the grind inside

sounds like *Number 9,*
your cappuccino vanilla mocha Urban Sunset on a Cypress Hill latte's
done! & Sorry ma'am, we don't have any vacancies for homes with 3
persons or more...

looks like a boarded up home in disrepair
next to a newly refurbished one
fresh coat of paint still glistening
looks like a rigid white girl's jawbones
& her pet pitbull's snarl

like a band of scraggly headed hopefuls
riding bikes 10 feet in the air
past a wrinkled old brown woman on her porch
looks like the look in that woman's eyes...
woulda swore she just seen an alien ship

looks like the look the hopefuls on bikes never give
if the word 'aloof' could campaign for a picture in the dictionary
it would put a Nikon 360 camera on those kids

tastes like... nothing
                    ...yet somehow still familiar...

like ya momma's favorite dish
but she forgot all the seasoning you know?
or too much of everything you never asked for
& when you got it, it ain't even much apply to you like...

a cappuccino vanilla mocha Urban Sunset on a Cypress Hill latte with a
side of...

kale

feels like an eerie sense of something
ain't quite right but how do I put my finger on it
when it keeps slipping from my grasp?
how identify what keeps disappearing?

like a floorboard slipped
from beneath your feet
then the whole room
then the whole house
then all of a sudden...
brand new floorboard
brand new house
but no more...

you

feels like a slow burn that only melts
all your skin off 10 years after the fact
feels like colonization in a velvet glove
like I think I'm getting fucked
but I'm not quite sure

feels like never getting to come out the kitchen
when company comes, like
been working in the kitchen my whole life
& they just up & hired a whole new staff
out the blue, just like that, told me my recipes
ain't good here no mo', told me the restaurant
patrons don't like my ingredients
said it wasn't *cappuccino vanilla mocha Urban Sunset*
on a Cypress Hill latte with a side of... kale enough

said they got some new cooks now
but I could always go apply at the shop
'round the corner
only wasn't no shop
'round the corner, told me

nice job Anna Mae, Uncle Ben
we sure do appreciate your service
just so happens it's not needed
around here anymore but leave your kids
your kids can stay, we've got a nice shiny
new building to teach them in
where they can learn all about our predecessors
like Marco Polo & Christopher Columbus
so one day, when they grow up, they may not always know
when we're gonna show up
but they'll always, always, always
know us when we get here

without a country

tell me where the revolutionaries go
to die silent deaths
when the fire they once funneled
through incinerator chests
dwindles into smoke signals
slipped from exhaust pipe lungs
vocal chords rusted with age-old complaints

the diatribes of dying tribes
tangled in their wired scribe
truths once wielded more adeptly
in hands less arthritic
now twist in forked fingers
wrenched wretched by dharma undone

once translucent glyphs
smudged into illegible scritch-scratch
on withering scrolls

tales of old & futures foretold
gilded in their jaundiced gaze
pupils of past times anything but paradise
when the gods rolled snake eyes on their lives
& forced them to shed dead skins
(or be wrangled lifeless by them)
& adopt new ones
to weather the foreign terrains
of new ages

where do the country-less go...?
when abandoned by societies that they fathered
bastardized by their own seed
when the nations' trumpets rise
& drown out adjacent whispers & roars
subsuming all surrounding sounds
in the gulfs of their mighty throats
transmogrifying the martyrs voice
into a nationalist anthem
puppet stringing in dollars
the righteous teenage tantrum

where do the young rebels go...?
when they are no longer here
to be entertained
or make minstrelsy of their pain-
paved-pathways towards nirvana

where do they land...
on what foreign sands?
in what loveless rooms bereft of eyes
on what sunless porch bereft of others
in what great cities bereft of village?

Grounded by Sky:
A Southern Epitaph

knowing that I walk atop the bones of my ancestors
in the shadow of their oppressors
towering statuesque above me

I cannot look down without feeling
the puzzled pieces of my past
beckoning me back together
cannot look up without feeling
the weight of history break me into pieces

I cannot leave this ground & feel whole
cannot stand it either
without its heavy sky
pummeling my dreams into nightmares

the ground is a haunt
is a restless cauldron of simmering spirits
bubbling over beneath the soles
of callous sojourners singed
by the heat beneath their feet
yet numb to the stories in its foment

the sky is riddled in dead eyes
the probing gaze of ghastly men
now ghosts cast into iron

who when flesh
owned men, women & children my kin
who when flesh
beat men, women & children my kin
who when flesh
raped men, women & children my kin
who when flesh
slaughtered, maimed, murdered
men, women & children that looked like me

I cannot leave this ground
where the scattered bones of my ancestry
lay namelessly
without tomb nor headstone
sans burial ground much less monument
& not feel the echoes of a chorus
of gnashing teeth testimonies
hissing at my heels

can not stand this ground
without feeling
the frozen laughter of gilded antebellum
the sky a glacier of silence
that yet speaks so loudly

if you dare to listen closely
you'll hear their names
whispering proclamations of self praise
from the perch of street signs
that hang like still nooses
suspended in time
lynching the esteem of listless passersby
the stories beneath their feet
& above their heads
having passed them by

yet the themes having ground their weight
into their subconscious
making of their minds infertile soil
insufficient to nourish the seeds of dreams
for the dead eyes have probed
& made lifeless the soil
the bones have spoken
but their voices have been muted
by the cast iron gaze above

I live in New Orleans
where the bones of my ancestors
beat the ground like a drum
bang Bamboula rhythms
through the soles that walk this land

I live in the South
where monuments to Robert E. Lee
PGT Beauregard & Jefferson Davis
stand taller than most homes
& the street signs
are noosed in the names of slavers

I cannot leave this ground & feel whole
cannot stand it either
& not feel history
trying to break me
on its cyclic wheel

star gazing: under the lens

the gaze is upon me
and I am all petri dish specimen
to be inspected
and made spectacle of

I am ancient skin under modern scanner
my flesh folding in forested mystique
beneath foreboding eye

baobab tree trunk
trumping your dry season
with hidden waters

so in this age of
modern wasteland and urban decay
you know not from whence comes this flow

...nor how deep runs this well...
didn't I tell you I've known rivers?

perhaps you weren't listening
too busy watching
for how star shine crept through me

it leaked from every crevice
poured through every pore
but you only noticed it in my teeth

from minstrel grin to platinum grill
or in the tapping of my feet
yes I've been dancing man, laughing man

have gyrated hip like knee jerk reaction
made snake of my spine and slithered
out of the confines of narrowed lenses

too slender to properly render the expanse
of my being, your scope too micro to hold
the infinity within my frame

your cameras have never been able to capture me

too much Africa for your aperture
too much astral for your projection
of black face upon me

my skin, as dark and vast
as the canvas of night itself
so yes, paint me in broad strokes

of your blurred perception
your star-crossed eyes
too riddled in fear-fueled awe

to notice the details of my composition
i wax precise as lines on vinyl when I shine
wane nebulous on the clouded
vision of unfit eyes

my rhyme arching back to a time
before invasive eyes knew me
so the flow be whirling dervish

to make my space a little more Rumi
and them ancient rivers swirl within
until my purpose consumes me

I'll till the muddled soil of my past
until my present blooms me

  . . .

when the woes of the world had me beat
i got down to it and made a song

my serpentine sounds slithered out my mouth
until the whole world sang along

  . . .

I have always been the black
I have always been the night
I birthed the stars
and I can swallow them
whole

acknowledgments

Thanks to all the awkward and/or straight up oppressive situations that resulted in me writing these poems. Thanks to Geoff Munsterman and Sam Gordon for looking so closely at and offering such thoughtful feedback on this body of work. Thanks to New Orleans theater companies Junebug Productions, ArtSpot, and KMDance whose productions commissioned 3 of these poems: "Education", "Sleeper Cell," and "When They Came for Me" respectively. Thank you to Pluck! for publishing "Post-Racial America."

And that's all I got on the publishing list folks. Cause honestly I've sucked at getting my own work out there over the last several years. So to that end, thanks to Next Left Press for being the first to publish a full-length project of mine. But I promise I'm gonna do better with getting more of my words out there in the future y'all. This work, my first in 10 years (my last was my self-published debut Blind Visionz), represents the reincarnation of a long lost literary journey towards healing and self-actualization. And now that the trains' revving back up, I'm not ever getting off.

Ever Ever. Thanks for hopping on with me. All Aboard!